I0797825

LIVING IN COLOR

COLOR IN CONTEMPORARY INTERIOR DESIGN

COLORING A ROOM OF ONE'S OWN

STELLA PAUL

"COLOR IS A VITAL NECESSITY. IT IS A RAW MATERIAL, INDISPENSABLE TO LIFE, LIKE WATER AND FIRE." [1]

FERNAND LÉGER (1881–1955)

The colors of the rooms we inhabit reflect us. They tell stories about identity, taste, and culture. Color permeates everything. Color provides more than a backdrop for living out our lives. It's central, ubiquitous in our surroundings as well as in our thoughts and dreams, equally driving everything from utilitarian functions, to emotional state, to spiritual expression. We perceive color through complex processes of physiological input and mental analysis. Great thinkers have devoted countless efforts to understanding its workings, yet we are constantly dazzled by new insights even as we are confounded by unsolvable mysteries. We attempt to harness color by constructing elaborate competing systems for its organization. We try to define the ineffable and translate the visual into language—ricocheting from evocative, near-poetical terms to dryly numerical symbols for communicating what we see. Even so, we don't see eye-to-eye. We can't be sure that what one person sees (let alone what one feels) is the same as another's perception. Nevertheless, we find immense pleasure in cocooning ourselves with luscious color and affirming its powerful allures—whether we seek in it vibrantly unbridled revelry, or measured intellectual restraint, or soothing evocations of tranquility. It has always been that way. No matter how far back in history, people ask color to work its magic in spaces that mean the most to them. Color speaks to us. What, then, on its most fundamental level, is color?

"COLORS ARE THE DEEDS AND SUFFERING OF LIGHT." [2]

JOHANN WOLFGANG VAN GOETHE (1749–1832)

Color is light. But we didn't always know that. It was revolutionary when Isaac Newton teased apart the spectrum's constituent wavelengths in 1666. When sunlight ("white light") passed through Newton's prism, the sunbeam bent at varying angles to reveal colors as separate rays, each with its own precise wavelength. Newton then clinched his argument by passing the colored rays through a second prism, recombining all the colors into reconstituted white light.

When light hits a surface, some wavelengths are absorbed while others are bounced back; the waves that are reflected back signal its color. To see color in its manifestation as light, it takes a complex interplay between the physics of light's behaviors, the physiology and mechanics of an individual's eyes, and the unique analysis by each person's brain.

We're not alone in seeing color. But other animals see things very differently, with vision apparatus unlike ours. Dogs see the world only through wavelengths that translate to yellow and blue. There's no red or green in their worldview. Some butterflies see worlds of color unattainable by us, having more elaborate color receptors than humans. We can distinguish about ten million colors. But the field of electromagnetic energy available to human vision is just a small swath of a much larger bandwidth. Energy transmitted as wavelengths that we can't see with our eyes extends through infrared and ultraviolet light. And some species not only see these realms invisible to us, but those "invisible" colors play enormous roles in survival and propagation. Snakes have access to infrared, seeing heat from warm-blooded prey. Birds and bees see ultraviolet markings on plants and flowers that depend on pollination: patterning invisible to us. The living world is color coded. Colors we see as well as those we can't perceive show what is delectable or poisonous, what or whom to avoid or approach, whether to be afraid or aroused. Survival depends on color. Some animals change their colors to match their circumstances. In under a second, octopi (although color-blind) transform their skin into colors mimicking their surroundings. Human beings can't do the same, but we can reflect our moods in our environments—through color we surround ourselves with.

"COLOR DECEIVES CONTINUALLY." [3]

JOSEF ALBERS (1888-1976)

After revealing light's color waves, Newton took the further step of schematizing his rainbow of colors—the spectrum—into an arrangement of seven discreet hues in specific order. More than 350 years later we still use his scheme: red, orange, yellow, green, blue, indigo, and violet. It's purely an abstraction. The electromagnetic field is continuous; boundaries are subtle and fluid. Why break the field into exactly seven hues? Why include two colors, blue and indigo, that are so similar? Newton imposed order. Among other ideals, his concept of color regulation mirrored organizing rules for musical octaves. Any form of color organization is an imposition of some form of ideal order. Newton wasn't the first. In antiquity, Aristotle had a color scale, too, to show his belief that colors were formed through mixtures of darkness and lightness. So white was at one end and its polar opposite, black, at the other. Blue lies close to black because it's seen as an extreme of darkness. Aristotle's concept endured even through Renaissance Europe, thousands of years later.

Philosophers, scientists, artists, designers, and poets in every century theorized about how to organize color into coherent systems—and how to create harmony. And with every inquiry, what looked unequivocal in one framework could easily be disputed in another. Johann Wolfgang von Goethe didn't accept Newton's seemingly objective physics. He published his own color theories, which he considered his most important work. Goethe insisted on subjectivity, organizing colors into "plus" and "minus" categories according to specific sensations. Every hue is a trigger, leading alternately to melancholia or serenity. Some colors excite quick, lively feelings; others make a restless, anxious impression; others are powerful, radiant, or "splendid." The idea that even before it's an aesthetic issue, color performance is a psychological one tantalized people long before Goethe and continues long after.

"FULL SATURATED COLORS HAVE AN EMOTIONAL SIGNIFICANCE I WANT TO AVOID." [4]

LUCIAN FREUD (1922-2011)

Color begins in the physical but ends up in the psyche. Can anyone rightly predict responses to color? Although people in every period try, eagerly wanting to universalize, color is impossible to pin down. Reactions to color are tinted by our associations from childhood and our habits, shared cultural preconditioning, and personal idiosyncrasies. Carl Jung saw color as a symbolic language that might be decoded like a cipher: red stands for blood, blue for the spiritual. But someone else could find red implies romance or privilege, or insist that blue means loyalty or melancholy. Green could suggest envy, but also nature. Piet Mondrian linked the color so strongly to landscapes (anathema for him when he was creating purely abstract art) that he went to great length to avoid even looking out windows that opened onto fields and trees. He didn't want to color his thoughts. For a while, Richard Diebenkorn eliminated blue from his palette for the same reasons—too redolent of landscape when trying to think about abstraction.

Many psychologists in addition to Jung have read into color keys to the unconscious, seeking ways to measure or define impacts. Max Lüscher's mid-century color test revealed basic personality traits through subjects' ranked color preferences to 73 color swatches. A strong preference to blue shows a need for peace and tranquility. A predisposition to black and red mean suppressed excitement, which threatens to discharge itself in aggressive impulses and emotional violence. It's the ultimate red flag: "what cannot be mastered will be destroyed." A lot of color psychology reveals more about the interpreter and his or her cultural milieu than about people in general, or even individual subjects. But the work goes on.

Studies to measure colors' powers to control behavior are often linked to workplace productivity or sales and marketing. Rooms with colored lighting or walls are assessed on the subjects' sense of elapsed time: supposedly overestimated in red environments. Red has also been judged to make things seem bigger and affect pulse and blood pressure. When quickening the pace is desirable, such as in a fast-food restaurant, red is supposed to attract, stimulate excitement and move consumers along. Buyer beware, though. Studies are as fluid and inexact as is the concept of decoding specific emotions engendered by color. Market research by color associations and producers of consumer goods make much of color forecasting, with competing annual predictions billed as newsworthy announcements—and cause for us to surround ourselves with new products to embody the present moment.

Color and well-being have been linked forever. One contemporary study of blue light claims it decreases suicidal impulses, and even prompted the installation of blue lighting in selected train stations in Japan. But color's curative powers are as elusive (and longstanding) as color's poetic powers. In antiquity, colored gemstones were thought to contain colored light, used to both diagnose and cure disease. Chromotherapy was in vogue thousands of years later, in the belief that colored light would alter bodily function. Actually, we still use blue light as therapy to break down bilirubin in jaundiced infants, but we can't claim in it any broader or more nebulous overall well-being.

"COLOR! WHAT A DEEP AND MYSTERIOUS LANGUAGE, THE LANGUAGE OF DREAMS."[5]

PAUL GAUGUIN (1848–1903)

No language is precise or poetically nuanced enough to adequately describe color. Our eyes can discern millions of colors, yet the average English-speaking nonspecialist might use about a dozen terms for talking about color. We hardly have the words to summon basic hue, let alone what happens to color when textured or coated surfaces make light (and color) change dramatically. What do we even mean by hue? If fifty people were to conjure up "red," Josef Albers famously said, there would be fifty different kinds of red in their minds' eyes, with no two alike. Fire-engine red, crimson, merlot, brick red, vermilion, oxblood—all red—look wildly different. We accept remarkably broad categories to bind together things that are diverse, rarely elaborating. From stridently saturated cobalt blue to the most brooding, deepest midnight blue to a wan, powdery sky blue: all are blue. Velvety matte black is totally different from crystalline, glossy black. Should we use the same word for them?

Whether we have many words or few to draw upon, the fact is that humans go to great trouble to create a name for something. And cultures label colors differently. The English word "blue" encompasses an ocean of different tints and shades, but they seem (to us) to share a kinship. In Russian, there are two distinct words for what we categorize as one. Lighter and darker blue are classified separately. In Navajo, one word encompasses all of green and blue together, but uses two separate words for different types of black. It seems that not every language even has words for color names; the Pirahã, a remote Amazonian tribe, have none in their lexicon. Assigning words to sensory experience is a translation, and the disparate ways cultures group and categorize colors speaks to different ways of looking at the world.

Sometimes we impose abstractions of language on visual experiences, and these labels eventually become accepted as fact-based givens rather than idea-based analogies. Do colors really divide into "warm" and "cool"? Red and orange are tacitly warm, and blue epitomizes cool. In reality this is flipped. A heated object starts out red-hot but will glow white-hot with higher temperatures, eventually reaching blue-hot. But color language is not literal; it's analogue. And it can't be denied that deep blue waters suggest refreshing coolness. In other words, whatever label we impose might be concurrently apt or not. Color is impossible to pin down.

Much effort has gone into attempts to communicate clearly what is meant when discussing colors, or matching them across media for commercial production. Color systems have proliferated for centuries, articulating relationships between colors by charting color ranges in diagrams that take the shape of scales, circles or wheels, triangles, or stars. Globes and more complicated three-dimensional models attempt to go a step further, even, in communicating about color, making clear that hue alone does not describe color. Colors have three attributes, and although they work together, each can be teased out as a separate characteristic: hue, value, and saturation. One of many systems, A. H. Munsell's 1905 "Color Notation" shows every hue's gradations in value (or brightness) as well as saturation (or purity) of color. Using complex mathematical formulae to organize the individual colors in their sequences, Munsell's ideal was to define standards that could be readily grasped across platforms. These systems weren't purely theoretical; Munsell stressed the need for a system in order to "avoid mistakes and disappointments" that were inevitable with the available fuzzy descriptors. He wasn't the only one. The Pantone color system, a large, fanning deck of precisely scaled color swatches, originally serviced the printing industry but soon took a broader mandate to encompass color description in all arenas. There have been many national color boards across the world, international bodies such as the C.I.E. (Commission International de l'Éclairage), and standard units in many commercial enterprises such as wall paint companies. Colorimeters and spectrophotometers can now measure and identify color characteristics to an unprecedented degree, in principle making it possible to unequivocally describe color.

But with all those tools at hand, we still turn to poetic language to label the colors we're drawn to. The birth of Marie Antoinette's son set off a decorating craze for a color called "Caca Dauphin," a hue redolent of the infant prince's soiled diapers. Today, paint companies lure twenty-first-century tastes with wall paints called "Life Lesson," "Dead Salmon," "Salty Tear," "Three Legs," and "Thread Needle," or some of many variants on breath, including "Elephant's Breath," "Mole's Breath," or "Wind's Breath." The words vaguely conjure mood (if not hue). Alternately, some names for paint colors strike references that are anything but vague: "Nacho Cheese," "Mayonnaise," "Cheese Powder," or "Bagel." Whether one wants to live in an ethereal world of breathy whisper or one that brazenly celebrates the most ordinary foodstuffs without sugar-coating their quotidian origins, we can find the products to shape our own ambience with color.

"EVERY ROOM HAS ITS GLOOM, THE GREAT THING IS TO FIND THE COLOR THAT WILL CUT THE GLOOM." [6]

GERTRUDE STEIN (1874–1946)

Color has always been central in designing spaces that are important to us. It can signal rank, ritual, and belief in addition to personal and cultural tastes and states of mind. All are embedded in the nuances of color just as clearly as they are communicated through scale (be it intimate or monumental), or proportion, or the vocabulary of formal and decorative elements.

An urge to paint walls is at our foundation of being. We don't know who they were, what they did inside the interior spaces they created, or why they colored caves' walls with browns, russets, blacks, and whites, but paleolithic individuals at the most liminal stage of our prehistory were already using color masterfully to articulate interior spaces. Earth's silica, clay, and iron oxides were coaxed from friable ocher rocks to create worlds of enchantment: anatomically detailed renderings of animals as well as human handprints. Although we can't understand these earliest records of spectacularly colored interior spaces, we can be awed by their beauty and their mysterious power as well as the technical skill these cave walls reveal.

Rendering colorful scenes of ritual or symbolic meaning—transforming interior walls into magical environments that tell mythic narrative stories or depict dreamy illusionistic landscapes—has been inextricable to shaping significant interior spaces in many periods throughout our history, and in many cultures. Wall treatment by ancient Egyptians, or Mayans, or Babylonians is richly colored. Walls of Roman antiquity or Renaissance Europe attest to color, too. Frescos, not flat wall color, made walls into vivid protagonists instead of an unobtrusive sideline. Excavations at Pompei in 1748 captivated people everywhere, revealing brilliant rooms frozen in time by Vesuvius's cataclysmic eruption in 79 CE. Not for the first time—and not for the last—contemporary attitudes about living with color took inspiration from rooms of the past. A taste for Pompeian red still reverberates. In truth, many of the historical spaces that spark tastes centuries (or millennia) later are altered by time. Rooms of the past are not always perfect time capsules of their periods. For example, Greek architecture was vividly colored, not white. Thousands of years wore away the colored surfaces. But that didn't stop centuries of taste-makers from embracing the purity of stark white, and creating new white spaces under the influence of an expression they considered ideal—even though historically inaccurate. Le Corbusier saw the gleaming white Parthenon and celebrated its transformation into something white, not colored: "Thank God, time got the better of it and I salute the reconquered monochrome." To strip away color has often stood for stripping away frivolity and excess—sometimes signaling moral and spiritual ideals. Such is the case with Protestant Reformation church interiors, where sober, unembellished white was embraced as the perfect expression of abstemious spirit. Colors (including white and black) are beacons of underlying thought. Just enter a medieval cathedral to be transported by stained-glass windows that narrate significance through colored light. Or consider the use of glazed tiles in the soaring interior of many mosques, where light and color embody ideals of harmony, reverence, and transcendence.

Where some cultural moments seem to call for stripping away color, others welcome it—sometimes even for the florid excess that it might represent. Walls in luxurious villas at Pompei are not only brilliant. They are lavish. Color can be expensive, especially Pompei's red walls made from cinnabar, a substance that came from far away, was difficult to mine and work with, and cost dearly. Red rooms seemed to be everywhere in newly excavated Pompei, but some of them were actually yellow in their time. Volcanic gases chemically changed pigments. Some of those rooms had also used less expensive shortcuts to making a red environment, by painting a thin red wash on top of a yellow surface. Other rooms are unmitigated cinnabar, and their color saliently reflects their inhabitant's wealth as well as taste.

Red is not alone as a mark of prestige. Purple has long histories across several media as a coveted substance that's hard to get, expensive, and even restricted by law in some periods. To be "born in the purple" isn't merely idiomatic. The offspring of reigning Byzantine rulers were literally born in a room clad with porphyry, a rare purple stone. Sourcing materials for colors' almost always tells an important story, whether it's about the cost of taste or breakthroughs in technologies that introduce new access to color of all kinds. Available materials (and colors) change in every period. The burgeoning new chemistry of synthetic color formulae in the nineteenth century changed public taste in every medium. Brighter greens, chrome yellows, and artificial ultramarine and other blues were newly available and affordable. The color of rooms changed accordingly. New synthetic binders and resins for paints and other products that fill our homes constantly push our tastes in new directions and offer new options for exploiting color behaviors. Textures and light-play metamorphose colors and ask us to equally consider color's core attributes of value and intensity in addition to its family of hue.

Our world is color coded both by nature and by human design. Color fulfills desires, telegraphs attitudes and tastes, and even controls behaviors. Is it any wonder that we ask color to play the lead in the spaces we care about deeply?

1. Fernand Léger, "Color is a vital necessity" from "Color in the World," *Functions of Painting*, 1938, translated edition of 1973, New York: Viking, p. 119.
2. Johann Wolfgang von Goethe, "Colors are the deeds" quoted in Arthur Zajonc, *Catching the Light: The Entwined History of Light and the Mind*, New York and Oxford: Oxford University Press, 1993, p. 210.
3. Joseph Albers, "Interaction of Color", 1963, Yale University Press, New Haven and London, p. 1.
4. Lucian Freud, "Full saturated colors have an emotional significance" quoted in exh.cat *Lucian Freud: Naked portraits, Werke der 40er bis 90er Jahre (Works from the 1940s to the 1990s)*, ed. Jean-Christophe Ammann et al, Frankfurt am Main, 2001.
5. Paul Gauguin, *The Writings of a Savage*, ed by Daniel Guerin, New York. quoted in the 1996 edition.
6. Gertrude Stein, "Every room has its gloom" from Gertrude Stein, *Everybody's Autobiography*, 1937, from New York: Random House 1973 vintage edition reprint.

A LIFE LIVED IN COLOR

INDIA MAHDAVI

I often define myself as a polyglot and polychrome, because I associate colors and cultures with ease. Colors have become my mode of expression precisely because they embody the artistic freedom that I seek. They are the light and shadow of all the souths from which I originate, and they relate the nostalgia of a paradise lost that sparks within me the desire to imagine others. Colors are like the consequences of my memories, of a woven heritage: my mother's Egypt, my father's Iran, our travels while I was still a child, the France we settled in, my own roaming as an architect and designer.

I believe that colors constitute our shared heritage, a common bond between all humans, a mark of our *Homo sapien* identity. Colors play an essential role in nature because they provide beauty, and, for me, beauty lies at the heart of our history: it is the driving force of evolution. I think that we underestimate the importance of color in our lives. It's not only about intelligence, strength, or size. I sometimes think that Darwin underestimated the role that beauty plays in the survival of species, in all species, humans, of course, but also animals and plants.

Color is also a mark of identification to recognize oneself, or to mark a sense of belonging to a group, a tribe, or a family. I became aware of this during my latest trip to Iran, when I visited one of its main carpet workshops. Color plays a crucial role: it allows each tribe to distinguish itself from others by assigning a specific color to their carpets, in the same way that Scottish clans have a distinct tartan pattern.

In my work, in all of my creations, I seek to find the colors of my childhood. It is this rediscovered nostalgia that moves me, that inspires me. I grew up in the United States as a child. I remember watching the Technicolor Tex Avery cartoons on television and their dazzling colors that sparkled in my eyes. It left a permanent mark on me—just like cinema did. The small and big screens are to me, an infinite source of color—and thus inspiration.

The use of color is natural to me, it has never been artificial. It's instinctive and felt—more than it is conscious. When I see a space for the first time, color emerges. It emerges like a feeling. I feel colors. I think my psyche, just as my body, are synesthetic: each color is related to an emotion, to a smell, to a gesture, to a vision, to an impression . . . It has become my expression.

I strive to create ephemeral memories of places, a memory that leaves a mark on the person who visits and discovers the spaces I create. When I design a space—whether it is a restaurant, a hotel, or a private residence that must become the owner's portrait—I seek to bring out a strong and accentuated identity. And the most direct and spontaneous way to achieve this is through color.

Certain colors belong to certain places. For the hotel Condesa in Mexico City, I instinctively chose turquoise. It was the neighborhood's most popular color. It was its very own identity. I simply could not have chosen another color than this very particular shade of blue, to which I gave another identity by using it in a very different context. When I choose a color, it's often for unobvious reasons. Colors bear ancient significations that are concealed and classical. I strive to give them a new meaning beyond their commonly accepted definition. I try to push them beyond their limits, beyond their boundaries while questioning tradition.

Colors help me to take possession of a place—to provoke its true nature. Hence I seek the "right color"—a perfect dialogue between a space and its color. It's a way of celebrating and revealing a space's true depth. For example, when Mourad Mazouz approached me to take over the design of his London restaurant Sketch, I was immediately surprised by the place's eclectic intensity. I felt overwhelmed. And then, the idea of pink came to mind. Pink as a dominant color that helped to restore the space's balance and bring freshness and lightness, a childish frivolity pushed to an extreme. This choice was meant to be temporary, as Mourad wanted to change the decor every two years. However, the Gallery at Sketch and its radical pink were so successful that this unexpected color became its hallmark and deep-rooted identity.

For more than twenty years, I've imagined places, spaces, objects, and stories with the help of color. They have naturally become my friends, my allies. I invite them in to every space and in every object. They follow me everywhere I go. The more, the merrier. Our infinite conversation isn't mundane nor is it nagging—I like them to fight, argue, have a conversation, then comfort each other, reconcile, and love each other again. Colors live in me—and with me. Colors are like words. Each association generates a different meaning, like in a sentence. Such-and-such association reinforces or tames their intensity. I often speak of my colors as an alphabet, a grammar. They are my secondary mother tongue.

To give a new meaning to colors, I carry two secret weapons at all times. My very own palette of paint, that I specifically created with Mériguet-Carrère—it has fifty-two cards, like a deck of playing cards. I also have a velvet palette, crafted by Pierre Frey, the great textile artisan. I named it "True Velvet," with David Lynch's movie in mind. Every card is composed of three velvets—including one that clashes with the other two, that interferes with it. This unusual discrepancy is very practical: it keeps my eye on guard, it helps me find alliances that seem impossible but that secretly provoke beauty.

In my line of work, I seek to celebrate joy, I want the places that I invent to carry energy. Color has the power to fight sadness. It isn't a coincidence if children and elderly people are attracted to color and energies. Children look around, they are born with their eyes wide open, seized by the power of color. Elderly people, those who have seen it all, only seek the most important, the strongest colors. In the end, all that is left is color. It kindles the burst of life that seizes the eye. My intimate relationship with color has allowed the public to recognize my spaces and my creations. Better still, color has allowed me to differentiate myself. To find a place that is mine.

They are my virtues, my sisters.
They're a part of my every day, of my creations.
They're dear to me, my colors.

LIVING IN COLOR

16 Living Room, New York City Apartment — New York, New York, USA — 2010
Barbara Dente (interior design); Jean Nouvel (architecture)

Kitchen, Panoramic Penthouse — New York, New York, USA — 2016
Workshop/APD

18 Dining Area, Art Dealer's Loft — Long Island City, New York, USA — 2008

Steve Blatz

Living and Dining Area, Art Dealer's Loft — Long Island City, New York, USA — 2008
Steve Blatz

20 Bathroom, Peach Farm Residence — East Hampton, New York, USA — 2014
Dekar Design

Entrance, Lakeside House — Wayzata, Minnesota, USA — 2013
Michelle Andrews

Bathroom, Brighton Residence — Brighton, Victoria, Australia — 2020
Golden

Bathroom, Lafayette Street Residence — New York, New York, USA — 2004
Solveig Fernlund and Neil Logan

Bedroom, Von Teese Residence — Los Angeles, California, USA — 2018
Dita Von Teese

26 Bedroom, Studio — Brooklyn, New York, USA — 2010

Snarkitecture

Entrance, Private Residence — Frankfurt, Germany — 2016
Joseph Dirand

Kitchen, Avenue Montaigne Apartment — Paris, France — 2017
Joseph Dirand

 Living Room, Greenwich Village Residence — New York, New York, USA — 2013
Rafael de Cárdenas

Bedroom, Park Avenue Apartment — New York, New York, USA — 2018
Thomas Pheasant Studio

32 Bedroom, Manhattan Apartment — New York, New York, USA — 2011
Jenny Dyer

Living Room, Belnord Apartment — New York, New York, USA — 2018
Rafael de Cárdenas

Dining Area, Penthouse Bunker — Berlin, Germany — 2008
Christian Boros

Living Room, Xanadune Residence — Southampton, New York, USA — 2019
Wesley Moon

Reading Nook, Vester Voldgade Residence — Copenhagen, Denmark — 2020
Studio David Thulstrup

38 Bedroom, Hidden Ridge Residence — Hidden Hills, California, USA — 2018
Martyn Lawrence Bullard

Living Room, Bel Air Residence — Los Angeles, California, USA — 2018
Sara Story Design

Living Room, Reflections Residence — New York, New York, USA — 2018
M.A. Bowers

Living Room, Park Avenue Apartment — New York, New York, USA — 2018
Thomas Pheasant Studio

Ann Pyne, McMillen

Family Room, Buckhead Residence — Atlanta, Georgia, USA — 2018
Suzanne Kasler Interiors

Living Room, Southampton Cottage — Southampton, New York, USA — 2012

Ann Pyne, McMillen

Living Room, Woodside Residence — Woodside, California, USA — 2016
Benjamin Dhong

Kelly Wearstler

50 Bedroom, Château Fourcas-Hosten — Bordeaux, France — 2013
Michael Coorengel and Jean-Pierre Calvagrac

Bedroom, Betsey Johnson Residence — Malibu, California, USA — 2016
Betsey Johnson

Yellow Room, The Farm — Sharon, Connecticut, USA — 2019
Michael Trapp

Bedroom, Cap Cana Residence — Cap Cana, Dominican Republic — 2011
Juan Montoya Design

 Living Room, London House — London, England, UK — 1987
Anthony Collett

Living Room, Fazenda Guariroba Residence — Campinas, São Paulo, Brazil — 2015
Sig Bergamin

Bedroom, Elias Residence — São Paulo, Brazil — 2000
Jorge Elias

 Bedroom, MJ Residence — Undisclosed Location — 2010
Studio Daminato

Living Room, Hotel Particulier Apartment — Paris, France — 2015
Roberto Peregalli and Laura Sartori Rimini, Studio Peregalli

Living and Dining Room, Pool House, Villa Peduzzi — Lake Como, Lombardy, Italy — 2019
Studio Daminato

Pamela Shamshiri

Studio, The Old Red Schoolhouse — Middletown, Rhode Island, USA — 2014
John Peixinho

Bathroom, Daniel Arsham Residence — Long Island, New York, USA — 2020
Snarkitecture

 Living Room, Casa Foa — Santiago, Chile — 2017
Grisanti & Cussen

Drawing Room, Parisian Pied-à-terre — Paris, France — 2006

Alidad

Dining Room, Manhattan Townhouse — New York, New York, USA — 2014
Laura Santos Interiors

Home Office, Juarez and Ploener Residence — New York, New York, USA — 2016
Christina Juarez and Company

Home Office, Fifth Avenue Apartment — New York, New York, USA — 2011

Robert Couturier

Bedroom, Elias Residence — São Paulo, Brazil — 2000
Jorge Elias

Janie Molster

Bedroom, Brooklyn Heights Townhouse — Brooklyn, New York, USA 2010
Kathryn Scott Design Studio

Kitchen, Château de Montigny — Normandy, France — 1999
Andrew Allfree

Master Bedroom, Trey Trust Residence — Los Angeles, California, USA — 2007
Stephen Samuelson, Plan A Architecture

Dining Room, Private Residence — New York, New York, USA — 2012
Jay Jeffers

Entrance, Franklin Hills Residence — Los Angeles, California, USA — 2019
Reath Design

Library, New York City Townhouse New York, New York, USA — 2013
Ann Pyne, McMillen

Steven Gambrel, S.R. Gambrel (interior design); Liederbach & Graham (architecture)

 Living Room, Sarise and Stephen Dweck Residence — Jersey Shore, New Jersey, USA — 2008
Stephen Dweck

Library, Palmolive Apartment — Chicago, Illinois, USA — 2015

Steven Gambrel, S.R. Gambrel (interior design); Liederbach & Graham (architecture)

Living Room, Pied-à-terre — San Francisco, California, USA — 2014
Thomas Britt

Thomas Britt

Library, Houston Residence — Houston, Texas, USA — 2013
Redd Kaihoi

Entry, Darlinghurst Apartment — Sydney, New South Wales, Australia — 2019
Greg Natale

Greg Natale

The Library, Park Avenue Apartment — New York, New York, USA — 2019
Cindy Adams

Doherty Design Studio

Meditation Loft, Trey Trust Residence — Los Angeles, California, USA — 2007
Stephen Samuelson, Plan A Architecture

Living Room, Asolo Residence — Asolo, Italy — 2018
Michela Goldschmied

Living Room, Jaipur Jewel Apartment — Rajasthan, India — 2010
Liza Bruce and Nicholas Alvis Vega

 Living Room, Chelsea Loft, Rashid Residence — New York, New York, USA — 2003
Karim Rashid

Entrance, Private Residence — Cabo San Lucas, Mexico — 2018
Ken Fulk

Living Room, Minimal Fantasy Apartment — Madrid, Spain — 2020
Patricia Bustos Studio

 Breakfast Room, Palm Beach Residence — Palm Beach, Florida, USA — 2016
Bunny Williams

Bedroom, Williams Residence — Beverly Hills, California, USA 2018
Kravitz Design in collaboration with Disco Volante

Child's Bedroom, A Slow Designed Home — London, England, UK — 2015
Suzy Hoodless

114 Bedroom, Private Residence — Long Island, New York, USA — 2010
Kelly Behun (interior design); Sawyer Berson (architecture)

Bedroom, Peter's House — Copenhagen, Denmark — 2015
Studio David Thulstrup

Child's Bedroom, Skok Residence — Lincoln, Massachusetts, USA — 2018
Mally Skok Design

Living Room, Le Palais Bulles — Théoule-sur-Mer, France — 1993
Patrice Breteau (interior design); Antti Lovag (architecture)

Living Room, Von Teese Residence — Los Angeles, California, USA — 2018
Dita Von Teese

Living Room, Kips Bay Show House — West Palm Beach, Florida, USA — 2020
Suzanne Kasler Interiors

Sitting Room, Southampton Residence — Southampton, New York, USA — 2013
Bunny Williams

Garden Room, Jaipur Jewel Apartment — Rajasthan, India — 2010
Liza Bruce and Nicholas Alvis Vega

Bedroom, Fredonia Residence — Los Angeles, California, USA — 2019
Nicolò Bini, LINE Architecture

Steven Gambrel, S.R. Gambrel (interior design); Arcologica Architecture (architecture)

Bedroom and Sitting Room, Hacienda Estate — Los Angeles, California, USA — 2004
Carrie Fisher

 Bedroom, Chelsea Loft — New York, New York, USA — 2014
Bruce Bierman Design

Den, Connecticut Saltbox — Connecticut, USA — 2018
Stephen Sills Associates

Bedroom, Pierre Apartment — New York, New York, USA — 2012
Atelier AM

Media Room, Palm Beach Residence — Palm Beach, Florida, USA — 2016
Bunny Williams

 Bedroom, Le Palais Bulles — Théoule-sur-Mer, France — 1993
Patrice Breteau (interior design); Antti Lovag (architecture)

Living Room, West Village Townhouse — New York, New York, USA — 2007
Steven Gambrel, S.R. Gambrel

Guest Room, Chesapeake Residence — Baltimore, Maryland, USA — 2018
Laura Hodges Studio

Living Room, Private Residence — Fayetteville, Arkansas, USA — 2009
Tobi Fairley Interior Design

Dining Room, Captiva Island Residence — Captiva Island, Florida, USA — 2008
Anthony Baratta

Bedroom, Château Fourcas-Hosten — Bordeaux, France — 2013
Michael Coorengel and Jean-Pierre Calvagrac

Andrew Howard Interior Design

Living Room, Southampton Residence — Southampton, New York, USA — 2013
Bunny Williams

Living Room, Greenwich Village Residence — New York, New York, USA — 2018
Steven Gambrel, S.R. Gambrel (interior design); HS Jessup (architecture)

 Entrance, Franklin Lakes Residence — Franklin Lakes, New Jersey, USA — 2013
Katie Ridder

Dining Room, Revivalist Mansion — Chicago, Illinois, USA — 2019

Steven Gambrel, S.R. Gambrel (interior design); Liederbach & Graham (architecture)

Family Room, Captiva Island Residence — Captiva Island, Florida, USA — 2008

Anthony Baratta

 Dining Room, Birch Castle — San Francisco, California, USA — 2014
Ken Fulk

Living Room, Macpherson Residence Miami, Florida, USA — 2019
Sawyer Berson

Sitting Room, The Lake House — Sonoma, California, USA — 2018
Ken Fulk

Home Office, Family Townhouse — Chicago, Illinois, USA — 2016
Steven Gambrel, S.R. Gambrel (interior design); Liederbach & Graham (architecture)

Hallway, Vacation Home — Bellville, Texas, USA — 2018
Redd Kaihoi

Home Office, Watch Hill Residence — Westerly, Rhode Island, USA — 2018
Studio Giancarlo Valle

Home Office, Family Townhouse — Chicago, Illinois, USA — 2016

Steven Gambrel, S.R. Gambrel (interior design); Liederbach & Graham (architecture)

 Dining Room, Fredonia Residence — Los Angeles, California, USA — 2019
Nicolò Bini, LINE Architecture

Sitting Room, Malvern Residence — Melbourne, Victoria, Australia — 2019
Doherty Design Studio

Dining Room, Park Avenue Residence — New York, New York, USA — 2017
Frank de Biasi and Gene Meyer

Family Room, Captiva Island Residence — Captiva Island, Florida, USA — 2008
Anthony Baratta

Bathroom, Casa Corbellini-Wassermann — Milan, Italy — 2019
Piero Portaluppi (interior design); Studio Binocle (restoration); Antonio Citterio (architecture)

 Living Room, Creole Cottage — New Orleans, Louisiana, USA — 2010
Carl Palasota

Carl Palasota

Bedroom, Townhouse — Chicago, Illinois, USA — 2015
Alessandra Branca

Bathroom, Beaulieu — Newport, Rhode Island, USA — 1992
Valerian Rybar

Garden Room, Creole Cottage — New Orleans, Louisiana, USA — 2010
Carl Palasota

James Aguiar and Mark Haldeman

Living Room, The Ensworth — Nashville, Tennessee, USA — 2016
Clary Collection

 Dining Room, Kips Bay Show House — New York, New York, USA — 2017
Ken Fulk

Screening Room, Villa Grigio — Palm Springs, California, USA — 2017
Martyn Lawrence Bullard

Salon, Château de Montigny — Normandy, France — 1999
Andrew Allfree

 Living Room, The Harrison — San Francisco, California, USA — 2016
Ken Fulk

Library, Château Fourcas-Hosten — Bordeaux, France — 2013
Michael Coorengel and Jean-Pierre Calvagrac

 Living Room, Arrowhead Farm Cottage — Long Island, New York, USA — 2000
James Morgan Topping

Dining Room, House in Tokyo — Tokyo, Japan — 2009
Mlinaric, Henry & Zervudachi (interior design); Kengo Kuma (architecture)

Bedroom, Ski Chalet — Montana, USA — 2018
Kylee Shintaffer

Ken Fulk

Living Room, Avalon Vista Residence — Newport Coast, California, USA — 2012
Craig Higgins

Reception Area, Ett Hem Hotel — Stockholm, Sweden — 2012
Studioilse

Entrance, California Craftsman Home — Palo Alto, California, USA — 2013
DLC-ID de la Cruz Interior Design

Bar, Urban Residence — San Francisco, California, USA — 2018
Martin Kobus, Kobus Interiors

 Bedroom, Tuscan Guesthouse — Arezzo, Italy — 2012
Roberto Baciocchi

Bedroom, Ett Hem Hotel — Stockholm, Sweden — 2012
Studioilse

 Sitting Room, Renwick Residence — New York, New York, USA — 2016
Eran Chen and Ryoko Okada, ODA

Study, Clinton Hill Brownstone — Brooklyn, New York, USA — 2015
Bespoke Only (interior design), Sarah Jacoby (architecture)

 Living Room, Alhadeff and Duzansky Residence — New York, New York, USA — 2017
David Alhadeff, The Future Perfect

Bedroom, West Village Townhouse — New York, New York, USA — 2013
Shawn Henderson Interior Design

Entrance, Medina Riad — Tangier, Morocco — 2007

Roberto Peregalli and Laura Sartori Rimini, Studio Peregalli

Living Room, At Home — Oslo, Norway — 2017
Studio Kråkvik & D'Orazio

Sarah Jacoby Architect

Home Office, Tapestry Penthouse — London, England, UK — 2017
Faye Toogood

Living Room, Beach Ryosha Residence — Del Mar, California, USA — 2020
Lucas Interior

Entrance, Fitzroy House — Melbourne, Victoria, Australia — 2016
Fiona Lynch Interior Design

DIRECTORY OF DESIGNERS

DIRECTORY OF LOCATIONS

INDEX

ACKNOWLEDGMENTS AND PICTURE CREDITS

PUBLISHER'S ACKNOWLEDGMENTS

The publisher would like to acknowledge the invaluable contributions of the following people, without whom this book would not have been possible. Tim Balaam, Vanessa Bird, Clive Burroughs, Julia Hasting, Melissa LeBoeuf, India Mahdavi, João Mota, Anthony Naughton, Celeste Ollivier, Stella Paul, Holly Pollard, Kate Sclater, Kim Scott, Hans Strofregen, and Anthony Tran.

PICTURE CREDITS

Note: On page 205, the artwork shown above the fireplace in the home of the founder of Design Gallery Galerie Provenance is a 1937 lithography by artist Benjamin Abramowitz. © Peter Aaron/OTTO: 103; © Brittany Ambridge/OTTO: 20; Photography by Irina Boersma, courtesy of David Thulstrup: 36; Photography by Henry Bourne, courtesy of Toogood: 29; Dave Brook: 112; Sharyn Cairns: 22, 214; Pascal Chevallier: 62; Justin Coit/Trunk Archive: 52; © Ty Cole/OTTO: 204, 211; © Roger Davies/OTTO: 39, 57, 59, 71, 75, 80, 82, 84, 92, 93, 100, 194; Adrian Dirand: 27; Mark Durling: 63; Tom Fallon: 61; Andrea Ferrari: 189; Joe Fletcher: 60; © Floto+Warner/OTTO: 26, 30, 40, 154; Albert Font: 37; Don Freeman/Trunk Archive: 188; Douglas Friedman: 119; Douglas Friedman/Trunk Archive: 21, 25, 38, 44, 67, 69, 105, 120, 151, 152, 156, 175, 180, 181, 184, 185, 187, 193, 196, 198, 213; Photography by Felix Forest, courtesy of Richards Stanisich: 109; Alfredo Gildemeister: 70; Tobias Harvey: 212; Laure Joliet Photography: 86; Dean Kaufman/Trunk Archive: 23, 107; © Stephen Kent Johnson/OTTO: 98, 116, 132, 133, 160, 166, 177, 200, 205; © Max Kim-Bee/OTTO: 31, 42, 113; © Nikolas Koenig/OTTO: 16, 18, 19, 76; Photography by Peter Krasilnikoff, courtesy of David Thulstrup: 115; Francesco Lagnese: 108, 134; © Francesco Lagnese/OTTO: 141, 165; Massimo Listri: 209; Thomas Loof/Trunk Archive: 34, 53, 66, 94, 117, 136, 143, 169; Spencer Lowell/Trunk Archive: 65; Mark Luscombe-Whyte/The Interior Archive: 56; Magnus Marding/Trunk Archive: 195, 201, 210; JC de Marcos @jcdemarcos: 106; © Michael Moran: 41; © Martin Morrell/OTTO: 28, 171; Nobuaki Nakagawa: 190; Photography by Helen Norman: 140; © Frank Oudeman/OTTO: 202, 215; Skye Parrott/Trunk Archive: 178; Photography by Paolo Petrignani, courtesy of Achille Salvagni Atelier: 95; Eric Piasecki: 73; © Eric Piasecki/OTTO: 51, 54, 55, 74, 78, 89, 91, 125, 127, 128, 138, 139, 147, 148, 149, 158, 161, 172, 173, 176, 192, 208; Rebecca Reid: 123; Coliena Rentmeester/Trunk Archive: 49; © Lisa Romerein/OTTO: 48, 87; Stefano Scata/The Interior Archive: 101, 155; Annie Schlechter/The Interior Archive: 77; Joe Schmelzer/Trunk Archive: 126; Jason Schmidt/Trunk Archive: 68, 142, 150, 168; Fritz von der Schulenberg: 121, 146; © Michael Sinclair: 179; Delfino Sisto Legnani and Marco Cappelletti: 170; Photography by Anson Smart, courtesy of Tamsin Johnson: 135; Photography by Anson Smart, courtesy of Greg Natale: 96, 97, 203, 207; Monica Steffensen: 197; Derek Swalwell: 99, 164; Martyn Thompson/Trunk Archive: 206; © Trevor Tondro/OTTO: 24, 110, 118, 124, 159, 162, 167; © David Tsay/OTTO: 145; Simon Upton/The Interior Archive: 72, 83, 90, 102, 104, 122, 153, 182; Frederik Vercruysse: 64; Wallo Villacorta: 33; © William Waldron/OTTO: 32, 35, 50, 85, 114, 129, 130, 144, 186, 199; © Björn Wallander/OTTO: 17, 43, 45, 46, 47, 58, 79, 81, 88, 131, 137, 157, 163, 174, 183; Joachim Wichmann: 111; Andrew Wood/The Interior Archive: 191.

BIOGRAPHIES

INDIA MAHDAVI

Architect, designer, and scenographer, India Mahdavi is based in Paris. Her studio, created in 2000, is known for the diversity of its international projects that explore the fields of architecture, interior design, scenography, and furniture and object design—all based in one single street in Paris, rue Las Cases. India Mahdavi is known for creating unique environments, combining a modern sense of comfort and elegance with color and humor—a cross-cultural ***art de vivre***. Polyglot and polychrome, India Mahdavi has become a signature, offering a special vocabulary that is joyful, cosmopolitan, and elegant all at the same time.

STELLA PAUL

Educated at Harvard University and the University of Southern California, Stella Paul currently lives in New York. At The Metropolitan Museum of Art for twenty-four years, Paul brought audiences and art together, fostering engagement, knowledge, and interpretation for visitors from scholars to students. She served as Museum Educator-in-Charge of Exhibitions and Communication, designing programs, lecturing, teaching, and writing. Before joining the Met, Paul ran Southern California efforts for the Smithsonian's Archives of American Art, a distinguished repository of documentary material and oral history resources.

With museum responsibilities across the widest sweep of chronology and culture, Paul explored connections revealed through broad interdisciplinary study—always with abiding attention to color. In recent years she's written about color in art, architecture, design, and other areas in which color fuels our thoughts and dreams. Her book, *Chromaphilia: The Story of Color in Art*, tracks colors' dazzling mysteries through case studies about materials and meaning spanning millennia. Paul's "I See a Red Door and I Want It Painted Black," introduces *Black: Architecture in Monochrome*. "Seeing Red, Everywhere" was released in *Red: Architecture in Monochrome*, and "Mapping the Colors of the Moon" is published in *The Color of the Moon: Lunar Painting in American Art*.

Phaidon Press Limited
2 Cooperage Yard
London E15 2QR

Phaidon Press Inc.
111 Broadway
New York, NY 10006

Phaidon SARL
55, rue Traversière
75012 Paris

phaidon.com

First published 2021
Reprinted in this compact format 2026

ISBN 978 1 83729 144 1 American English Edition
ISBN 978 1 83729 196 0 UK English Edition

A CIP catalogue record for this book is available from the British Library and the Library of Congress.

Commissioning Editor: Virginia McLeod
Production Controller: Sarah Kramer
Design: Hyperkit
Typesetting: Cantina

Printed in China